Optavia Cookbook

100+ Lean & Green and Fueling Snack Ideas.

The Advanced Optavia Diet Cookbook With New Recipes to Make Your Weight Loss Easier.
Healthy and Yummy High-Protein Recipes on a Budget.

By

Olive Bennett

© Copyright 2021 by Olive Bennett - All rights reserved.

No part of this publication may be reproduced, stored, copied, or shared by any means, electronic or physical, or used in any manner without the publisher's prior written consent.

TABLE OF CONTENTS

Introduction	7
Cookbook	11
Lean & Green	13
Poultry	15
Chicken Fajita Lettuce Wraps	17
Mediterranean Chicken Salad	18
Spicy Chicken with a Mint Sauce	19
Turkey Cucumber Rolls	20
Balsamic Chicken	21
Coconut-Lime Chicken & Snap Pea Slaw	22
Traditional Chicken Curry	23
Baked Chicken with Lemon & Veggies	24
Skinny Pineapple Chicken with Cashews	25
Chicken Roulades	26
Chicken Wings with Creamy Broccoli	27
Chicken and Cabbage Dish	28
Slow Cooker Turkey Breast	29
Mediterranean Turkey-Stuffed Peppers	30
Turkey Salad Lettuce Wraps	31
Meat	33
Roast Pork Tenderloin	35
Flank Steak & Chimichurri Sauce	36
Southwestern Steak Salad	37
Cilantro-Lime Steak	38
Beef Lettuce Wraps	39
Flank Steak with Horseradish Dressing	40
Braised Pork in Sweet Soy Sauce	41
Ribeye & Brussels Sprouts Skillet	42
Slow Cooker Pulled Pork	43
Pork Souvlaki	44
Fish	45
Teriyaki Salmon	47
Cilantro Salmon	48
Chia Crusted Tuna with Mango Sauce	49

Lemon Garlic Herb Salmon	50
Coconut Salmon Fish Sticks	51
Brazilian Fish Stew	52
Roasted Chili-Lime Cod	53
Soy-Ginger Marinated Tilapia	54
Grilled masala fish	55
Shrimp and Cauliflower Grits	56
Tuna patties	57
Greek Fish Florentine	58
Mahi-Mahi with Pineapple & Red Peppers	59
Sesame Coconut Halibut & Shirataki	60
Seared Halibut with Microgreens Salad	61

Vegan — 63

Spinach and Tofu Scramble	65
Seitan & Black Bean Stir-Fry	66
Bean Burgers	67
Bean & Squash Stew	68
Creamy Cauliflower	69
Cloud Bread	70
Falafel Bites	71
Cottage Deviled Eggs	72
Tofu Stir-Fry	73
Tofu Pumpkin Curry	74

Fuelings — 75

Smoothies — 77

Red Velvet Smoothie	79
Chocolate Protein Smoothie	80
Strawberry Cheesecake Smoothie	81
Super-Green Smoothie	82
Piña-Colada Smoothie	83
Su-Pear Smoothie	84
Lemon Poppy Smoothie	85
Orange Smoothie	86
Filling Raspberry Smoothie	87
Salted Caramel Potion	88

Protein Bars — 89

Coffee Protein Bars	91
Vanilla Nougat Protein Bars	92

Cinnamon Roll Protein Bars	93
Pepperoat Bars	94
Noat-Bake Protein Bars	95
Pumpkin Protein Bars	96
No-Bake Nana-Cake Bars	97
Peanut Butter Bomb	98
No-Bake Coconut Bars	99
Dark Chocolate & Sea Salt Bars	100
Desserts	**101**
Berry Cheesecake Muffins	103
Mouse Dessert	104
Protein Chia Pudding	105
Double Chocolate Protein Fudge	106
Energy Bites	107
Protein Oreos	108
Chickpea Cookie Dough	109
Molten Chocolate Mug Cake	110
Tiramisu Protein Pancakes	111
Protein Peanut Butter Cups	112
Soups	**113**
Broccoli-Parmesan Chicken Soup	115
Vegan Broccoli Cheddar Soup	116
White Chicken Chili	117
Tomato Soup	118
Pea and Ham Soup	119
Cauliflower Soup	120
Cheesy Ham Chowder	121
Potato Soup	122
Crab Soup	123
Corn Chowder	124
Quick Snack Tips	**125**
Celery and Peanut Butter	127
Poppy Crackers	128
Frozen Yogurt Blueberries	129
Apple Muffins	130
Sweet Potato Chips	131
Breakfast Sandwiches	132
Beef and Cheddar Roll-Ups	133
Skinny Burrito in a Jar	134

Overnight Oats	135
Roasted Chickpeas	136

Shopping List — 137

Conclusion — 139

Introduction

"Don't worry. I know what I'm doing. I have Olive Bennett's Optavia Cookbook."

I know you're exhausted from all the weight loss options and workout plans. To see the results you want, you have to eat correctly. You can go crazy on the treadmill or at the squat rack if you don't know how to correctly nutrient your body. If you overeat, your body stores the extra energy that it doesn't burn as fat. If you eat too little, your body holds on to that fat because it gets into starvation mode and protects you from losing weight.

Your body won't lose fat just unless you find the right calories and macronutrients it needs. What the body needs is balance. A diet, that provides you with a variety of foods and won't make you feel restricted.

When you´re dieting, it's highly recommended to eat mostly whole foods, lean protein, and avoid any cheat meals in the beginning. The first reason is that the brain will forget about the cheat meals and won't crave them later. The second is, of course, the body image. The body will respond to the quality nutrition it gets and will start cooperating. There's no doubt in this if you're dedicated and don´t cheat (at least at the beginning).

Although Optavia Diet is a low-calorie diet, it is a high protein diet, so it will satisfy you and help you build or hold on to muscle.

Lean and Green recipes consist of 5 to 7 ounces of cooked lean protein, 3 servings of non-starchy vegetables, and possibly up to 2 servings of healthy fats. In the initial 5&1 Plan, having 6 meals per day, you will have less than 100 grams of carbs, which might be the reason for the fast weight loss for some individuals.

However, as a nutritionist and passionate cook, I'm not a fan of the initial 5&1 Plan because I think it's too restrictive. For a dieter who´s been trying to lose weight, it might be very stressful to eat so little and the person´s body won´t let the fat go, but opposite, it will save it. But I'm a fan of the 3&3 Plan because it gives more variety to your meals.

If you´re just starting with your weight loss, with or without the Optavia diet, I recommend you start slow and jump directly into the 3&3 Plan. Don´t worry, at the beginning, only replacing the food with healthier options, will have a big impact on your health and your body will react to it. You will feel better, healthier, lighter without having to sacrifice.

If you have already gone through the initial phase, you might know it´s not so easy to maintain as a lifestyle regime. That´s why the diet is divided into a few stages. However, the original diet requires you to buy packed, powdered, overpriced food that one might not consider delicious. You have to search for hacks to make the meals tastier, however, you´re losing the number one benefit of these meals, which´s supposed to "save you time". Therefore, I like to help you with my knowledge and cooking experience and give you more ideas for the healthy Lean and Green recipes as well as some quick snacks that you can consider as fueling – but whole and healthy.

With this book, you will have more variety in your fuelings as well. You can either replace them all or continuously replace the purchased, processed food for the meal and snack ideas that I provide, step by step. As stated above, to be healthy and get weight loss results, you need to eat enough! With 3&3, you can find the balance you need to live healthily but still satisfied.

If your goal is to either maintain your new weight or you're aiming for a slower, healthy, and sustainable weight-loss without starving yourself, you're in the right place. This cookbook gives you more ideas on healthy recipes to create at home, helping you stick to the diet and live a balanced, healthy, and happy lifestyle.

I wish you good luck & Bon Appetit!

Olive Bennett

Cookbook

Lean & Green

Poultry

Chicken Fajita Lettuce Wraps

⏲ 45 minutes 🍴 4 servings

Ingredients:

16 oz chicken breast slices
2 bell peppers
2 teaspoons olive oil
2 teaspoons fajita seasoning
1 tablespoon fresh lime juice
romaine salad
1/2 cup non-fat Greek yogurt

Instructions:

Preheat oven to 400°F.

Cut all ingredients into small slices and combine them all, except the salad, in a large seal bag. Mix well to coat evenly.

Move the bag content onto a foil-lined baking sheet and bake 25 to 30 minutes until the meat is thoroughly cooked.

Serve on romaine salad and top off with a halved tablespoon of Greek yogurt. Serve with more leafy vegetables.

Mediterranean Chicken Salad

25 minutes 6 servings

Ingredients:

28 oz chicken breast
2 tablespoons butter
1 cup sliced cucumber
6 cups Romaine salad
10 Kalamata olives
1 pint of cherry tomatoes
1/3 cup low-fat feta cheese
2 tablespoons lemon juice
Salt and pepper

Instructions:

Preheat your oven or grill to about 350°F.

Season the chicken with salt, butter, and black pepper. Roast or grill chicken for about 25 minutes, or until it reaches an internal temperature of 165°F. Once your chicken is cooked, remove it from the oven and keep aside to rest for about 5 minutes. Slice to any width you prefer.

Combine all the salad ingredients and toss everything together gently.

Serve the chicken over the Mediterranean salad.

Spicy Chicken with a Mint Sauce

⏲ 30 minutes 🍴 4 servings

Ingredients:

4 (7 oz) chicken breasts
1 tablespoon cayenne pepper
1 tablespoon smoked paprika
2 teaspoons ground cumin
2 teaspoons ground mustard seeds
2 teaspoons ground fennel
1 teaspoon black pepper
2 teaspoons salt
Olive oil

Parsley-Mint Sauce:
1 ½ cups mint leaves
¾ cup parsley
6 cloves garlic
2 serrano chiles
2 tablespoons honey
2 tablespoons Dijon mustard
1 cup olive oil
Salt and pepper

Instructions:

Preheat the grill to the maximum.

Mix cayenne pepper, cumin, mustard, fennel, pepper, and salt together.

Sprinkle the chicken with a few teaspoons of oil. Rub a little bit of the mixture onto the breasts and place it on the grill. Grill for about 5 minutes until golden brown and slightly burned. Turn your breasts over and continue cooking for another 5 minutes.

For the sauce, put mint, parsley, garlic, and serranos in a blender and mix well. Add honey and mustard and process until combined. Slowly add the olive oil while the blender is running.

Put the mixture in a bowl and add a few tablespoons of cold water to the desired consistency - season with salt and pepper to taste.

Place the chicken on a plate and drizzle with a little parsley-mint sauce. Let it rest for 5 minutes.

Serve another scoop of sauce on the side.

Turkey Cucumber Rolls

⏱ 15 minutes 🍴 2 servings

Ingredients:

2 cucumbers
¼ cup green pesto
4 oz turkey ham
4 oz mozzarella
1 bell pepper
1/2 cup spinach
salt and pepper

Instructions:

Slice the cucumbers lengthwise into 2 mm slices. Place them on parchment paper and dry them carefully with a paper towel.

Spread pesto on each slice evenly and add turkey and mozzarella cut into same-sized pieces. Add peppers cut into thin slices and spinach. Season it with salt and pepper to taste.

Roll up and put the seam down. You can also stick a toothpick through for easy appetizers! Serve with extra pesto or low-carb sauce of choice.

Balsamic Chicken

⏲ 15 minutes + marinate 🍴 4 servings

Ingredients:

20 oz chicken breast
¼ cup olive oil
¼ cup balsamic vinegar
2 cloves garlic
1 tablespoon Italian seasoning
Salt and pepper

Instructions:

In a bowl, mix oil, vinegar and add all the seasonings.

Put the chicken in a bowl and add the marinade. Coat well and refrigerate for at least 1 hour, and ideally overnight. Remove from the marinade.

Preheat oven to 400°F.

Grease a baking dish with oil and place the chicken breast on the baking dish and bake for about 40 minutes. Or you can insert a meat thermometer in the center of the meat, and when it reads 165°F, the chicken is ready.

Coconut-Lime Chicken & Snap Pea Slaw

⏲ 45 minutes 🍴 4 servings

Ingredients:

2 (8 oz) chicken breasts
2 tablespoons sesame oil
1 tablespoon fresh ginger
3 tablespoons fresh lime juice
10 oz snap peas
4 oz snow peas
2 scallions
1 tablespoon olive oil
2 tablespoons coconut cream
1/2 cup cilantro
salt and pepper

Instructions:

In a bowl, mix together sesame oil, ginger, 1 1/2 tablespoons of lime juice, and 1/2 teaspoon of salt. Add snap peas, snow peas, and chopped scallions, and mix carefully.

Cut each breast lengthwise in half and make four thin cutlets. Then pound each of them into 1/4 inch thick pieces.

Heat oil in a skillet on medium-high. Season the meat with 1/2 teaspoon salt and pepper and cook in batches for 2 minutes on each side, until golden brown and cooked through.

Place the chicken on plates. Remove pan from the heat and stir in coconut cream and remaining lime juice, scraping up any browned bits. Spoon this creamy mixture over the chicken.

Put the cilantro into the pea mixture and serve on top of the chicken.

Traditional Chicken Curry

⏲ 30 minutes 🍴 6 servings

Ingredients:

24 oz chicken breasts
1 cup chicken broth
2 tablespoons olive oil
1 onion
6 cloves garlic
1 red chile
2 tablespoons ginger
1 tablespoon garam masala
1 tablespoon ground coriander
2 teaspoons sweet paprika
2 tablespoons tomato paste
1/4 cup zero-fat yogurt
Cauliflower rice and chopped cilantro
salt and pepper

Instructions:

Heat the olive oil in a large pot on medium-high heat. Add onion and cook, occasionally stirring, until it becomes translucent.

Reduce heat to medium and cook 3 to 4 more minutes until tender.

Add in diced garlic and chile. After 1 minute, add finely grated peeled fresh ginger, garam masala, coriander, paprika, and ½ teaspoon salt. Cook for 2 minutes, stirring constantly. Lastly, stir in tomato paste and cook 2 more minutes.

Season chicken with salt and pepper, add to the pot and cook for 5 minutes until it turns from pink to light-brownish.

Stir in chicken broth and let it simmer covered for about 5 to 8 more minutes until the meat is cooked through.

Stir in yogurt and serve over rice, sprinkled with cilantro if desired.

Baked Chicken with Lemon & Veggies

⏲ 60 minutes 🍴 4 servings

Ingredients:

4 (5 oz) chicken breasts
8 oz pumpkin
1 bunch asparagus
1 teaspoon honey
1/4 cup olive oil
1 lemon
2 garlic cloves
1 tablespoon Dijon mustard
1 teaspoon Italian seasoning
1/4 teaspoon ground cumin
Fresh cilantro
Salt and pepper

Instructions:

Preheat your oven to 420°F. Season the breasts on both sides with salt and pepper.

Put the chicken breasts in a lightly oiled baking pan. In another bowl, mix the lemon zest and juice, garlic, mustard, Italian spices, cumin, cilantro, and honey. Add in 1/4 cup oil until combined. Sprinkle with a little bit of salt and lots of fresh pepper.

Put the pumpkin and asparagus around the chicken and drizzle the chicken and veggies with the sauce. Cut the lemon into slices and place a piece on top of each chicken.

Cover the baking pan with foil and bake it in the oven for 40 minutes. For the last 5 minutes, remove the foil and bake to crisp up.

Serve immediately, garnished with more cilantro.

Skinny Pineapple Chicken with Cashews

⏲ 20 minutes 🍴 4 servings

Ingredients:

24 oz chicken breasts
1 tablespoon canola oil
1 cup pineapple
2 garlic cloves
1 tablespoon fresh ginger
2 tablespoons rice vinegar
2 teaspoons sriracha sauce
1/2 teaspoon sesame oil
2 tablespoons soy sauce
2 teaspoons corn starch
1/2 cup cashews
Cauliflower rice
Salt and pepper

Instructions:

Heat the canola oil in a large skillet over medium-high heat. Add the chicken cut into small pieces to the skillet and season with salt and pepper to taste. Cook for about 7 minutes.

Mix two minced garlic cloves, minced ginger, rice vinegar, sriracha, sesame oil and soy sauce, and any pineapple juice if reserved (1 small cup).

In another small bowl, whisk together corn starch and 1/4 cup water until a smooth slurry is formed.

Add the sauce to the chicken, then stir in the cornstarch slurry. Heat over medium heat, continually stirring, until thickened for about 3 minutes.

Add half a cup of cashews and diced pineapple to the skillet.

Serve over cauliflower rice garnished with fresh cilantro.

Chicken Roulades

⏲ 35 minutes 🍴 4 servings

Ingredients:

4 (5 oz) chicken breasts
2 cloves garlic
1 lemon (zest and juice)
1/2 cup Parmesan
1 cup baby spinach
3 tablespoons olive oil
2 cups cherry tomatoes
1/4 small red onion
2 tablespoons red wine vinegar
salt and pepper

Instructions:

Heat oven to 450°F.

Pound chicken breasts into thin cutlets. In a bowl, mix chopped garlic, lemon zest, and parmesan.

Lay 8 spinach leaves on each chicken cutlet, then sprinkle garlic mixture on top. Roll the cutlets up and secure with a toothpick, placing them in parallel to the seam to make turning roulades easier. Sprinkle the roulades with salt and pepper.

Heat 1 tablespoon of oil in a big, oven-friendly skillet on medium-high. Cook the roulades seam side down for 5 to 7 minutes, turning until browned from all sides. Then transfer the roulades to the oven and bake until cooked through up to 10 minutes.

While roulades roast, stir together tomatoes, onion, red wine vinegar, 2 tablespoons of olive oil, and salt and pepper to taste.

Take the roulades out of the oven and drizzle lemon juice on top of them.

Serve the marinated tomatoes with the chicken. Enjoy!

Chicken Wings with Creamy Broccoli

⏲ 50 minutes + marinate 🍴 4 servings

Ingredients:

Chicken wings:
48 oz chicken wings
½ orange
¼ cup olive oil
2 teaspoons ground ginger
1 teaspoon salt
¼ teaspoon cayenne pepper
Creamy broccoli:
24 oz broccoli
1 cup light mayonnaise
¼ cup fresh dill
salt and pepper

Instructions:

Preheat the oven to 400°F.

In a small bowl, mix juice and zest from the orange with oil and spices. Marinate the chicken wings in the marinade. Put aside for at least 20 minutes or longer.

Lay the wings on a greased baking dish and bake on the middle rack for about 45 minutes or until the wings are thoroughly cooked and crispy.

Meanwhile, cut the broccoli into small florets and parboil in salted water for a few minutes until they soften. Make sure they won't lose their bright green color. Strain the broccoli and let it cool slightly. Then add the remaining ingredients.

Serve and enjoy!

Chicken and Cabbage Dish

⏲ 50 minutes 🍴 4 servings

Ingredients:

4 chicken drumsticks
2 tablespoons avocado oil
1 teaspoon paprika
1 teaspoon garlic powder
1 teaspoon onion powder
1 teaspoon parsley
14 oz cabbage
1 (4 oz) red onion
2 tablespoons olive oil
1 cup mayonnaise
salt and pepper

Instructions:

Preheat oven to 425°F. Spray a baking sheet with a cooking spray.

Add avocado oil, paprika, garlic, and onion powder, and chopped parsley to a large zip-lock bag and seal. Add the chicken and coat in the seasoning.

Place chicken on the baking sheet and bake for 40 to 45 minutes.

Shred the fresh cabbage with a mandolin and serve it on a plate.

Chop the onion and serve it on the plate next to cabbage, together with the rotisserie chicken and mayonnaise.

Drizzle about a teaspoon of olive oil on each plate's cabbage and add some salt and pepper to taste. Easy peasy!

Enjoy!

Slow Cooker Turkey Breast

⏲ 3 hours 20 minutes 🍴 6 servings

Ingredients:

48 oz turkey breast
1 1/2 tablespoons butter
1 small onion
1 large carrot
1 stalk celery
1 cup chicken broth

1 tablespoon fresh rosemary
1 tablespoon fresh thyme
1 Zest of 1 small lemon
1 tablespoon all-purpose flour
Salt and pepper

Instructions:

Add chopped onion, carrots, and celery to the bottom of your slow cooker. Pour in 1/2 cup of chicken broth.

In a bowl, combine rosemary, thyme, salt, pepper, and lemon zest. Rub the herb mixture over the skinless and boneless turkey breast.

Put the turkey on top of the vegetables in the slow cooker. Cover and cook for about three to three and half hours on a high setting, or until a thermometer inserted into the thickest part of the breast registers 165°F.

Preheat the oven broiler. Transfer the cooked turkey breast to a foil-lined baking sheet. Save the liquid in the slow cooker and broil the turkey for about 10 minutes.

Drain the liquid from the slow cooker into a measuring cup and add broth to it to make 2 cups. In a saucepan, melt butter and whisk in flour. Cook for 2 to 3 minutes, whisking constantly. Slowly pour in the drippings and broth, whisking until the gravy thickens and until no lumps remain.

Slice the chicken and serve immediately with the gravy.

Mediterranean Turkey-Stuffed Peppers

⏲ 30 minutes 🍴 4 servings

Ingredients:

18 oz turkey breast
4 oz mozzarella
4 big red peppers
4 tablespoons olive oil
1 small onion
2 garlic cloves
2 teaspoons ground cumin

8 mushrooms
1 (14 oz) can tomatoes
2 tablespoons tomato purée
2 chicken stock cubes
handful of oregano leaves
green vegetables

Instructions:

Heat oven to 374°F. Cut the peppers lengthways, remove the seeds and core but keep the stalks. Rub the red peppers with olive oil and season well. Put on a baking tray and bake for 15 minutes.

Heat 2 tablespoons of olive oil in a pan over medium heat. Fry the minced turkey for 3 to 5 minutes, stirring well to break up the chunks. Then move it into a plate.

Wipe out the pan and heat the other two tablespoons of olive oil over medium-high heat. Add the onion and garlic, stir-fry for 2 to 3 minutes and then add the cumin and mushrooms and cook 2 minutes longer.

Add the meat back to the pan and add in chopped tomatoes and tomato purée. Grind in the stock cube and cook for 5 minutes, then add the oregano and seasoning.

Remove the peppers out from the oven and fill them with as much of the mince as you can. Top them with cheese and return to the oven for 15 mins until the cheese turns golden.

Carefully slide the peppers on your plate and serve with your favorite greens, blanched, boiled, or steamed. Enjoy!

Turkey Salad Lettuce Wraps

⏲ 35 minutes 🍴 5 servings

Ingredients:

1 1/2 cups roasted turkey meat
1/4 cup mayonnaise
1/4 cup sour cream
1/2 teaspoon garlic powder
1/4 cup cheddar cheese
1 scallion
Lettuce or romaine salad
Salt and pepper

Cranberry Mustard:

1 1/2 cups cranberries
2/3 cup water
2 tablespoons mustard
1 1/2 tablespoons chicory syrup
Salt

Instructions:

Shred the roasted turkey meat into small pieces.

In a bowl, mix the mayonnaise, sour cream, garlic powder, salt, and pepper.

Add the shredded turkey, sharp cheddar cheese, and chopped scallions. Mix to combine and coat the chicken. Cover and set aside in the refrigerator.

In a small pan, combine the cranberries and water. Heat on medium heat until the cranberries have softened, then add the mustard and chicory syrup and stir to combine. Cook for 2 to 3 minutes.

Remove the cranberry mixture from the heat and blend the ingredients with a hand mixer until completely smooth. Add salt to taste and let cool in the refrigerator.

Place about a 1/3 cup of the turkey in each lettuce leaf and drizzle the cranberry mustard on top.

Serve and enjoy!

Meat

Roast Pork Tenderloin

⏰ 30 minutes 🍴 5 servings

Ingredients:

36 oz pork tenderloin
2 tablespoons balsamic vinegar
2 tablespoons extra virgin olive oil
4 cloves garlic
steak seasoning blend
2 sprigs fresh rosemary
2 sprigs fresh thyme

Instructions:

Preheat oven to 500°F.

Cut the silver skin and connective tissue off tenderloin with a very sharp thin knife.

Place tenderloin on a non-stick baking sheet with a rim. Drizzle tenderloin with a few tablespoons of balsamic vinegar and rub the vinegar into the meat. Then drizzle with olive oil, just enough to coat the meat. Make small cuts into the tenderloin with a knife and disperse chunks of cracked garlic cloves into them.

Combine steak seasoning blend or coarse salt and pepper with rosemary and thyme and rub the meat with the mixture. Roast in a hot oven for 20 minutes.

Let meat rest, transfer to a carving board, slice, and serve.

Flank Steak & Chimichurri Sauce

⏲ 30 minutes + marinate 🍴 4 servings

Ingredients:

16 oz skirt steak
1/4 cup olive oil
2 tablespoons red wine vinegar
1 1/2 tablespoons water
1/2 cup chopped parsley
1/2 cup chopped fresh basil
3 tablespoons oregano
3 tablespoons garlic
3 tablespoons shallots
Salt and pepper

Instructions:

Blend all the flavoring and seasoning ingredients in a food processor. The sauce should be a course in texture and assertive in flavor. Adjust to taste.

Leave half cup of the sauce aside to use for serving.

Place the steak in a bowl, pour the remaining sauce over it, and then coat it from all sides. Marinate for at least 30 minutes. If you keep it marinating longer, close it in the air-tight container in the refrigerator, but make sure to take it out 30 minutes before cooking.

Preheat the grill to medium-high. Sweep any excess chimichurri sauce off the steak, pat dry, and season it with salt and pepper.

Cook the steak on the grill for about 6 to 7 minutes on each side for medium-rare.

Move the cooked steak on a cutting board, cover loosely with a foil, and let it rest for about 5 minutes. Slice thinly and serve with the reserved sauce.

Southwestern Steak Salad

⏱ 50 minutes 🍴 4 servings

Ingredients:

4 (5 oz) ribeye steaks
4 tablespoons Butter
1 tablespoon vegetable oil
4 cloves garlic, thyme
2 hardboiled eggs
6 cups of lettuce mix of your choice
1/2 cup corn
1/2 cup black beans
1/2 bell pepper
1/4 red onion

1/2 cup queso fresco
1/2 cup cilantro leaves
Vinaigrette:
1 lime
1/3 cup olive oil
2 cloves garlic
1 tablespoon Dijon mustard
1/2 teaspoon ground cumin
1/2 teaspoon chili powder
Salt and pepper

Instructions:

Pour all the ingredients for vinaigrette into a small bowl and whisk until combined. Set aside.

Slice the steak into 1-in slices and bring it to room temperature. Pat dry and season with salt and pepper. Bring your skillet to smoking hot and cook the steak for about 2 to 3 minutes on each side. Then push the steak to a side and add butter, garlic and thyme, but be careful, the thyme will sputter. When the butter is melted, spoon it on the steak and cook to your preferred doneness, about 2 minutes each side. Remove from the skillet and let it rest for 5 to 10 minutes, so it absorbs its own juices.

In another big bowl, mix the lettuce mix, beans, corn, thinly chopped red onion, bell pepper, and crumbled queso fresco. Add a few tablespoons of the vinaigrette and mix very carefully with salad tongs or a fork. Layer the salat on the plates and add the steak and egg slices on top. Top off with cilantro and enjoy!

Cilantro-Lime Steak

⏲ 40 minutes + marinate 🍴 4 servings

Ingredients:

16 oz shoulder steak
1 cup lime juice
1 bunch cilantro
½ teaspoon curry powder
3 scallions
Salt and pepper

Instructions:

In a blender, combine lime juice, lime zest, cilantro, curry powder, and scallions and process.

Place the steak in a zip-lock bag and pour half of the marinade in to coat the steak. Let the steak marinate for 30 to 45 minutes. Reserve the other half of the marinade.

Lightly oil hot grill and heat it to medium-high. Remove steak from marinade, shaking off the excess. Add salt and pepper to taste.

Grill the steak for about 8 to 10 minutes per side for medium-rare, until browned. Then transfer to a cutting board and let it rest for 5 minutes before slicing. Slice against the grain into thin slices.

Season reserved marinade with salt and pepper and serve with sliced steak.

Beef Lettuce Wraps

⏱ 20 minutes 🍴 2 servings

Ingredients:

Beef:
8 oz ground beef
1/2 cup onion
1 tablespoon fresh ginger
1 garlic clove, chopped
3 tablespoons soy sauce
2 tablespoons lime juice
Red pepper flakes
1 teaspoon sesame oil
6 large lettuce leaves

Peanut Sauce:

1/3 cup peanut butter
1/4 cup peanuts
1/4 cup soy sauce
2 teaspoons sesame oil
3 tablespoons sugar
2 tablespoons lime juice

Instructions:

Preheat a medium-sized skillet over medium-high heat. Cook the beef for about 10 minutes, carefully drain any excess fat.

Add the onion, ginger, garlic, soy sauce, lime juice, red pepper flakes, and sesame oil to the beef and stir to combine. Reduce the heat and let the ingredients cook for 5 more minutes.

To make the peanut sauce, mix all the ingredients in a blender and blend until smooth.

Layer the lettuce leaves on a plate and scoop the beef mixture into each lettuce cup.

Drizzle 2 teaspoons of peanut sauce over each lettuce wrap, garnish with cilantro and peanuts if desired, and enjoy!

Flank Steak with Horseradish Dressing

⏲ 30 minutes + refrigerate 🍴 2 servings

Ingredients:

2 (7oz) flank steaks
1/3 cup olive oil
2 garlic cloves
2 tablespoons red wine vinegar
1/3 cup soy sauce
Salt and pepper
Dressing:

1 lemon zest
1/4 cup freshly grated horseradish
1/4 cup fresh parsley
1 tablespoon lemon juice
1 tablespoon olive oil
Salt

Instructions:

Combine the marinade ingredients and put the marinade in a large zip-lock bag or a plastic container with a lid. Add steak and seal the bag and shake well until the steak is well covered. Set aside for at least 3 hours in the fridge.
While the steak is marinating, mix all the dressing ingredients, and set aside. Preheat the grill to high heat. Take the meat out from the bag and sprinkle it thoroughly on all sides with coarse salt and freshly ground pepper.
Place the steaks on the grill and cook for about 5 minutes on each side for a medium steak.
When the steak is done to the desired doneness, remove it from the grill and place it on a cutting board. Cover with a foil and let it rest for 10 minutes. Before serving, cut the side steak into pieces and drizzle with the lemony-horseradish dressing on top.

Braised Pork in Sweet Soy Sauce

⏲ 40 minutes 🍴 4 servings

Ingredients:

32 oz pork loin
2 tablespoons olive oil
1 tablespoon garlic and ginger paste
1 tablespoon olive oil
1 tablespoon sesame oil
1/2 cup soy sauce
4 tablespoons xylitol
1 1/2 cup water
1 tablespoon chili garlic sauce
2 green onions

Instructions:

Cut the meat into 1-inch pieces and sauté in a pan for about 3 minutes over medium-high heat. The meat has to turn from pink to brown.

In a bowl, combine the rest of the ingredients. Then pour the mixture over the pork and bring to a boil. When it starts to boil, lower the heat and let it cook for 30 minutes uncovered. Stir it occasionally until there are only about 3 tablespoons of sauce on the pan.

Garnish with green onions. Serve over veggies or cauliflower rice.

Ribeye & Brussels Sprouts Skillet

⏲ 35 minutes 🍴 2 servings

Ingredients:

14 oz beef Ribeye Steak
12 oz Brussels sprouts
1 teaspoon olive oil
1/2 teaspoon pepper
2 teaspoons fresh parsley
3/4 teaspoon all-purpose seasoning
1/4 cup Manchego cheese
1 tablespoon fresh lemon juice

Instructions:

Cut Brussels sprouts into halves and toss them with oil and 1/4 teaspoon pepper. Set aside.

Combine parsley, seasoning, 1/4 teaspoon of pepper, and press evenly on the beef.

Heat a large skillet over medium heat. Place steak in skillet and distribute Brussels sprouts around the meat. Cook steak 14 to 16 minutes for medium-rare (145°F) to medium (160°F), turning steak and stirring sprouts occasionally. Remove steak from the skillet and keep it somewhere warm.

Cover skillet and continue cooking sprouts 5 minutes or until they become crispy. Add Manchego cheese and lemon juice to skillet and mix to coat well. Season with salt to taste.

Cut the steak into thin slices and serve with Brussels sprouts. Enjoy!

Slow Cooker Pulled Pork

⏱ 7 hours 45 minutes 🍴 4 servings

Ingredients:

48 oz pork shoulder roast
1 tablespoon paprika
1 teaspoon garlic powder
1 teaspoon xylitol
1 cup barbecue sauce
1/4 cup water
1 teaspoon salt

Instructions:

In a small bowl, mix paprika, garlic powder, xylitol, and salt.

Spray slow cooker with cooking spray. Rub the seasoning mixture on pork and make sure to cover it completely. Place the pork in the slow cooker and pour water around.

Cover, and cook on low heat 7 to 8 hours. To speed it up, set the slow cooker to high heat and let it cook 3 to 4 hours, until very tender.

When cooked, put the pork on a cutting board and let it rest a little until it's cool enough to handle. Using two forks, shred the meat into shreds.

Clean the slow cooker and respray it with cooking spray. Return the shredded pork to the slow cooker and stir in the barbecue sauce.

Cover and let it cook on high heat setting up to 15 minutes.

Serve in lettuce wraps or Optavia-friendly side dish.

Pork Souvlaki

⏲ 60 minutes + refrigerate 🍴 4 servings

Ingredients:

20 oz pork tenderloin
3 lemons
1/3 cup fruity olive oil
4 garlic cloves
2 tablespoons oregano
2 teaspoons salt
1/2 teaspoon black pepper

Instructions:

Cut the pork tenderloin into small chunks and put them in a big plastic freezer bag.

Mix the fruity olive oil with the juice of 3 lemons. Stir in the garlic, oregano, salt, and pepper, and pour the marinade over the tenderloins in the bag. Seal the bag tightly, removing as much air as possible, and keep it in the fridge for at least 2 hours, but preferably overnight.

Heat a grill to medium-high. Remove the pork from the marinade and get rid of the marinade. Stir the meat on metal or wooden skewers that have been soaked for at least 20 minutes.

Grill the pork until browned, for 10 to 15 minutes, turning every few minutes. Transfer to a plate, cover with a foil, and let it rest for 5 minutes.

Sprinkle with parsley, another squeeze of lemon if you like, and serve with veggies of your choice.

Fish

Dietitians highly recommend incorporating fish in your diet at least once or twice a week. These lean fish recipes are perfect to spice up your diet plan, make it more versatile and flexible while staying in the high protein, low carb, moderate fat ratio, using only wholefood ingredients.

Teriyaki Salmon

⏲ 30 minutes 🍴 4 servings

Ingredients:

16 oz salmon
1 teaspoon cayenne pepper
4 teaspoons teriyaki sauce
2 cups zucchini
4 cups cabbage
2 teaspoons olive oil
Salt and pepper

Instructions:

Sprinkle the raw salmon with cayenne pepper or paprika and baste with the teriyaki sauce.

Broil it for about 7 minutes in a preheated broiler about 4 inches under the broiler. Remove from oven and wrap in tin foil until ready to serve.

Chop up the zucchini and cabbage. Sauté the zucchini and cabbage in olive oil in a pan until slightly brown. Season with salt and pepper.

Serve the salmon on top of the veggies.

Cilantro Salmon

⏲ 50 minutes + refrigerate 🍴 4 servings

Ingredients:

16 oz salmon
1-1/2 cups cilantro
1 tablespoon lemon juice
1 tablespoon hot red pepper sauce
1/2 teaspoons cumin
1/4 teaspoons salt
water

Instructions:

In a blender, combine cilantro, lemon juice, hot red pepper sauce, cumin, and salt, and add about 1/4 cup water for a puree consistency. Put the marinade in a zip-lock bag and add salmon, squeezing the excess air out of the bag and seal. Mix to coat the salmon and refrigerate for at least 1 hour or more.

Preheat oven to 400 °F.

Spray a baking dish with a non-stick cooking spray. Place bell pepper slices in a single layer on the baking dish and bake for 20 minutes. Turn the peppers after the first 10 minutes to cook from the other side.

Drain the salmon and get rid of the marinade. Place salmon on top of the pepper and bake 12 to 14 minutes. Turn the salmon once.

Serve salmon over the peppers.

Chia Crusted Tuna with Mango Sauce

⏲ 40 minutes 🍴 2 servings

Ingredients:

Tuna:
2 (5 oz) tuna fillets
1/8 teaspoon ground black pepper
1 tablespoon whole chia seeds
1 teaspoon canola oil
Mango Sauce:
1/2 cup chopped fresh mango
1 tablespoon snipped fresh cilantro
1 teaspoon lime juice
Balsamic Glaze:
1/4 cup xylitol
1/4 cup balsamic vinegar
1/4 cup water

Instructions:

In a small pan, combine xylitol, balsamic vinegar, and water. Reduce the heat and bring to a boil. Let it simmer uncovered for 10 to 12 minutes or until the mixture reaches the consistency of maple syrup. Stir regularly. Let it cool completely, so the mixture thickens as it cools.

Preheat oven to 425°F. Meanwhile, prepare the mango sauce, mixing the ingredients in a mixer and set aside.

Sprinkle tuna with the pepper. Spread chia seeds on a plate and press each tuna fillet into the chia seeds to evenly coat one side of the fillet.

Place the tuna chia sides up on a foil-lined baking pan coated with canola oil. Roast for about 12 minutes, until tuna is firm to touch and an instant-read thermometer inserted in centers registers 145°F. This time do not turn tuna over during roasting. When ready, remove from the oven and let it stand 2 to 3 minutes before serving.

Drizzle the plates with about a tablespoon of the balsamic glaze and top with the tuna fillet. Gently pour the salsa over the tuna. Store the remaining glaze in the refrigerator for another use.

Lemon Garlic Herb Salmon

⏱ 25 minutes 🍴 4 servings

Ingredients:

4 (5 oz) Wild Salmon Fillets
3 oz Ghee
1 Lemon
1 tablespoon Fresh Parsley
1 teaspoon Fresh Dill
1 Clove garlic
Salt
White Pepper

Instructions:

Preheat oven to 400°F.

Put ghee, lemon zest and lemon juice, parsley, dill, chopped garlic, salt, and pepper in a small bowl. Melt in the microwave for about 40 seconds and stir until combined.

Place the salmon fillets on a baking sheet lined with parchment paper.

Coat the salmon with the lemon ghee mixture, evenly spreading it over the tops of each fillet.

Bake in the oven on the top rack for 10 to 12 minutes, until salmon is cooked.

Serve and enjoy!

Coconut Salmon Fish Sticks

⏰ 30 minutes 🍴 4 servings

Ingredients:

Cooking spray
12 oz salmon filets
1/4 cup coconut flour
1/2 teaspoon salt
1/4 teaspoon pepper
1 cup coconut flakes
1/2 teaspoon garlic powder
1/4 cup parmesan
1 egg
1/4 cup fresh parsley
1/4 cup plain Greek yogurt

Instructions:

Preheat oven to 425°F. Put a baking rack in the middle of a baking sheet and spray it with a cooking spray. Cut the salmon into about a half-inch thick sticks.

In a bowl, whisk coconut flour, salt, and pepper and set aside.

In another bowl, mix the coconut flakes, garlic powder, and parmesan.

In the third bowl, whisk together the egg and two tablespoons of water. Line these three bowls and salmon - salmon, flour, egg, and coconut.

Dredge each of the fish pieces in the flour mixture, then in the egg mixture, and last in the coconut mixture and press in until all sides are well-coated. Place on the prepared baking rack. If you need more of any of the mixtures, feel free to add.

Lightly spray the top of the fish sticks with spray and bake in a preheated oven for 10 to 12 minutes, or until the outsides are slightly brown and crunchy.

Sprinkle the fresh parsley on the fish sticks just before serving and serve with Greek yogurt as a dip.

Brazilian Fish Stew

⏲ 45 minutes 🍴 4 servings

Ingredients:

36 oz cod
2 tablespoons lime juice
2 tablespoons fresh ginger
2 tablespoons olive oil
3 cloves garlic
2 teaspoons red pepper
1 onion
1/2 yellow bell pepper

1/2 red bell pepper
2 cups tomatoes
2 yellow plantains
1 teaspoon paprika
1 (14 oz) can coconut milk
1/2 cup bone broth
1/2 cup fresh cilantro

Instructions:

Add the cod fillets, lime juice, and ginger to a shallow bowl, mixing gently to wrap the cod and divide the ginger. Set aside and let marinate until you start with the rest of the stew.

Heat olive oil in a pot over medium heat. Add garlic, crushed red pepper, chopped onion, and chopped pepper and sauté for 5 to 8 minutes. Add sliced tomatoes and plantains and stir, cook for another 2 minutes.

Transfer the cod from the marinade to the Dutch oven and place the pieces of cod in the vegetables. Sprinkle with salt and pepper. Discard the marinade. Mix pepper, broth, and coconut milk in a Dutch oven. Reduce heat to low heat, cover, and cook for 10 minutes until the fish is easily peeled off. Stir in the coriander and serve immediately.

Roasted Chili-Lime Cod

⏲ 20 minutes + refrigerate 🍴 4 servings

Ingredients:

4 Cod Fillets
2 Teaspoons Paprika
2 Teaspoons Dried Parsley
1 Teaspoon Oregano
1 Teaspoon Chili Powder
1 Teaspoon Garlic Powder
1/2 Teaspoon Cumin
1/2 Teaspoon Salt
1/2 Teaspoon Freshly Ground Black Pepper
1/4 Teaspoon Cayenne Pepper
4 Tablespoons Olive Oil
2 Tablespoons Ghee
2 Limes

Instructions:

Preheat the oven to 450°F.

First, combine all of the spices. Brush the cod filets with 2 tablespoons of olive oil. Then, coat them very well with all the seasoning. Refrigerate the filets for at least 30 minutes or overnight.

Place the cod fillets on a foil-lined baking sheet and roast in the oven for 10 to 12 minutes. You know the fish is cooked through when the fillets will flake easily.

In a small saucepot, melt ghee and 2 tablespoons of olive oil. Add in lime zest and juice from 2 lemons and mix.

Serve the cod overtop of your preferred veggies and drizzle with the lime butter.

Soy-Ginger Marinated Tilapia

⏲ 20 minutes + marinate 🍴 4 servings

Ingredients:

20 oz tilapia fillets
¼ cup tamari
2 tablespoons chicory syrup
1 tablespoon sesame oil
1 tablespoon lime juice
1 tablespoon ginger
1 scallion

Instructions:

Line a baking tray with parchment paper.

In a bowl, stir together the tamari, chicory syrup, sesame oil, lime juice, grated ginger, and scallion. Add fish to the marinade and coat them thoroughly. Let the fish marinate for at least 15 minutes.

Preheat broiler. Layer the fish fillets on the baking tray and spoon a few tablespoons of the remaining sauce over them.

Place the tray at least 3 inches away from the broiler and cook for 10 to 12 minutes, until the fish flakes easily with a fork.

Serve immediately with zucchini noodles or other preferred veggies.

Grilled masala fish

⏱ 20 minutes 🍴 4 servings

Ingredients:

4 (5 oz) coley
olive oil
1 clove of garlic
fresh coriander
2 teaspoons turmeric
2 teaspoon chili powder
1 teaspoon ground coriander
2 teaspoons ground cumin

4 tablespoons mango chutney
4 tablespoons Greek yogurt
Coriander salad:
baby gem lettuce
4 spring onions
2 fresh red chilies
1 lemon

Instructions:

Preheat the grill to a high temperature and line a baking tray with foil. Brush it with a little bit of oil.

Put the fish on the tray. Grind the chopped garlic and coriander stalks to a paste with a pestle and mortar and stir in the dried spices and 4 tablespoons of olive oil and coat the fish with the herb paste.

Lower the grill down to medium and grill the fish for 4 minutes from each side – it's done when it flakes easily.

Meanwhile, prepare the salad. Cut the lettuce, chop the spring onions, deseed and slice the chili, and cut the lemon into wedges.

In another bowl, mix the coriander leaves, baby gem, spring onion, and most chili, with a squeeze of lemon juice, a splash of oil, and some seasoning.

Serve the salad on a plate, place the fish on top and spoon the chutney on top. Sprinkle with the reserved chili, then serve with the yogurt, naan, and remaining lemon wedges.

Shrimp and Cauliflower Grits

⏲ 20 minutes 🍴 2 servings

Ingredients:

16 oz shrimps
1/2 tablespoons Cajun seasoning
Cooking spray
1 tablespoon lemon juice
1/4 cup chicken broth
1 tablespoon butter
2 1/2 cups finely riced cauliflower
1/2 cup cashew milk
2 tablespoons sour cream
1/3 cup cheddar cheese
1/4 cup scallions
salt

Instructions:

In a large bowl, toss the shrimps and Cajun seasoning together.

Spray a big skillet with a cooking spray and heat over medium heat. Cook the shrimp for about 3 minutes per each side, until it becomes pink. Then add the lemon juice and chicken broth, scraping any bits from the bottom of the pan. Let it simmer for 1 minute and set aside.

In another skillet, heat butter over medium heat. Add the cauliflower and cook for 5 minutes. Add cashew milk and a bit of salt to taste.

After another 5 minutes of cooking, remove from the heat and mix in the sour cream and cheese until they melt.

Serve the cauliflower and shrimp over it and top it off with chopped scallions.

Tuna patties

⏲ 20 minutes 🍴 4 servings

Ingredients:

4 (5 oz) cans tuna
1 egg
1/3 cup almond flour
2 medium green onions
2 tablespoons fresh dill
1 tablespoon lemon zest
1/4 cup light mayonnaise
1 tablespoon freshly squeezed lemon juice
2 tablespoon avocado oil
Salt and pepper

Instructions:

Mix all ingredients except the avocado oil until combined. Then form 8 patties from the batter.

In a skillet, heat a tablespoon of avocado oil over medium heat. Add as many of the tuna patties as you can fit and cook them until golden for 3 to 4 minutes on each side.

Place on a paper towel and repeat with the remaining oil and patties.

Top with mayonnaise and sprinkle with lemon zest.

Greek Fish Florentine

⏲ 25 minutes 🍴 4 servings

Ingredients:

4 (5 oz) bass fillets
10 grape tomatoes
2 cloves garlic
2 tablespoons parsley
1 lemon
4 large shallots
2 tablespoons olive oil
16 oz baby spinach
1/2 cup low-fat feta cheese

Instructions:

Preheat oven to 350°F.

Put fillets and tomatoes in a glass baking dish, season with garlic and parsley, and drizzle with lemon juice. Cover the dish with foil and bake for 15 to 20 minutes, until the fish is opaque and flakes easily with a fork.

Sauté shallots in olive oil for 1 minute in a medium skillet on high heat. Then, reduce heat to medium and add spinach, cooking 5 more minutes. Add feta cheese and mix until melted and evenly distributed.

Serve 3/4 cup spinach-feta mixture on each plate and put one fillet on top. Top it off with grape tomatoes.

Mahi-Mahi with Pineapple & Red Peppers

15 minutes | 4 servings

Ingredients:

4 (5 oz) mahi-mahi fillets
2 teaspoon olive oil
2 cups fresh pineapple
1 red bell pepper
2 tablespoon fresh chives
Salt and pepper
lettuce

Instructions:

In a large skillet, heat oil on medium-high. Season Mahi-Mahi with salt and black pepper from both sides. Add the fillets to the skillet and cook for 1 minute per side, until they become golden. Then remove from pan and set aside.

Add chopped pineapple and bell pepper to the skillet and cook on medium heat for 2 to 3 minutes, until soft. Stir occasionally.

Add Mahi-Mahi back to the skillet, cover with foil and cook for the last 2 minutes until Mahi-Mahi is tender and steaming under foil.

Serve with lettuce or other preferred green veggies.

Sesame Coconut Halibut & Shirataki

⏱ 30 minutes 🍴 4 servings

Ingredients:

4 (5 oz) halibut fillets
1/4 cup shredded coconut
2 tablespoons sesame seeds
1 teaspoon coconut oil
1/2 red onion
1/2 red and yellow bell pepper
2 cloves garlic
3 cups shirataki mushrooms
8 oz shirataki noodles

1/2 cup vegetable broth
4 teaspoon tamari sauce
1 tablespoon fresh ginger
3 cups sugar snap peas
1 teaspoon fresh lemon juice
3 tablespoon fresh cilantro
cooking spray
Salt and pepper

Instructions:

In a small bowl, combine coconut and black or white sesame seeds. Coat halibut from both sides in the mixture, pressing slightly. Season with salt and black pepper.

Spray a big skillet with cooking spray and heat on medium heat. Cook halibut for 4 minutes from each side until golden and fish flakes easily with a fork. Move the fish to a plate and cover it to keep it warm.

Wipeout skillet quickly and heat oil on medium-high. Cook onion, bell peppers, mushrooms, and chopped garlic, stir until softened for about 3 minutes.

Add shirataki noodles, broth, tamari, and ginger and bring to a boil. Cook just about 2 minutes, until noodles become tender and liquid has reduced by half.

Stir in the sugar snap peas and cook until tender-crisp. Lastly, stir in lemon juice.

Serve Shirataki mix with halibut and garnish with cilantro.

Enjoy!

Seared Halibut with Microgreens Salad

⏱ 25 minutes 🍴 4 servings

Ingredients:

4 (6 oz) halibut steaks
2 kiwis
1/4 cucumber
3 cups fresh strawberries
1/2 lemon
1/4 teaspoons ground cinnamon
1/8 teaspoon ground cayenne pepper
1/3 cup fresh basil leaves
1/3 cup fresh mint leaves
6 cups assorted microgreens
Cooking spray
Salt and pepper

Instructions:

In a big bowl, mix chopped kiwi, cucumber, strawberries, lemon juice, 1 tablespoon of olive oil, salt, and pepper to taste. Combine gently, cover, and set aside.

Sprinkle halibut from all sides with cinnamon, cayenne pepper, and a pinch of salt and black pepper, gently rubbing spices into the steaks.

Heat a big skillet on medium-high and lightly spray with cooking spray. Cook halibut 4 minutes on each side until it becomes flaky and opaque throughout. Remove from heat and cover. Set aside.

Add basil and mint leaves to the kiwi mixture and mix to combine.

Serve on a plate in layers, microgreens, halibut, and kiwi mixture.

Enjoy!

Vegan

Spinach and Tofu Scramble

⏲ 10 minutes 🍴 2 servings

Ingredients:

2 tomatoes
2 cloves garlic
3/4 cup mushrooms
1 cup spinach
2 1/2 cups tofu
1/2 teaspoon soy sauce
1 teaspoon lemon juice
salt and pepper

Instructions:

Spray a medium-sized skillet with a cooking spray and heat over medium heat.

Add the tomatoes, garlic, and mushrooms and sauté for 2 to 3 minutes.

Reduce heat to and add tofu chopped to small pieces, spinach, soy sauce, and lemon juice. Cover with a lid and cook for the other 5 to 7 minutes, stirring occasionally. Sprinkle with salt and pepper.

Seitan & Black Bean Stir-Fry

⏲ 25 minutes 🍴 4 servings

Ingredients:

Stir-fry:
4 (5 oz) marinated seitan pieces
1 tablespoon arrowroot
2 tablespoons vegetable oil
1 red pepper
10 oz pak choi
2 spring onions
Shirataki noodles

Sauce:

14 oz black beans
½ cup xylitol
3 garlic cloves
2 tablespoons soy sauce
1 teaspoon Chinese five-spice powder
2 tablespoons rice vinegar
1 tablespoon smooth peanut butter
1 red chili

Instructions:

For the sauce, drain and rinse black beans and tip half of the can into a mixer with the rest of the ingredients, and add ¼ cup of water. Blend until smooth. Pour into a saucepan and heat up for about 5 minutes, until it thickens slightly.

Drain the seitan pieces, pat dry with a kitchen towel, mix them with the arrowroot, and set them aside.

Heat wok to a high temperature, add oil and seitan. Stir-fry for around 5 minutes until golden brown. Then remove the seitan from the wok using a slotted spoon and set aside.

If the wok is dry, add 1 teaspoon of vegetable oil. Add the shallots and stir-fry until soft. Throw in the chopped peppers, the second half can of beans, pak choi, and chopped spring onion. Cook for about 3 minutes, then add the seitan back to the pan and stir in the sauce. Bring to boil for 1 minute.

Serve with cooked shirataki noodles.

Bean Burgers

⏰ 20 minutes 🍴 3 servings

Ingredients:

1 can (15 oz) beans
1/2 onion
1 teaspoon garlic powder
1 teaspoon onion powder
1/2 teaspoon seasoned salt
1/2 cup almond flour
2 slices keto bread crumbled

Instructions:

Spray a large skillet with cooking spray and heat over medium heat. Add the onions and sauté until soft, about 3 – 5 minutes.

Meanwhile, add the black beans into a big bowl and mash until only a few chunks remain. Add chopped onions, garlic powder, onion powder, salt, and the crumbled keto bread. Add the flour in slowly, a couple of tablespoons at a time, to prevent clumping.

Divide into three portions and form into patties. Re-coat the skillet you used for onions in cooking spray and fry the patties until slightly firm, 2 – 3 minutes on each side.

Bean & Squash Stew

⏱ 30 minutes 🍴 2 servings

Ingredients:

1 (15 oz) can red kidney beans
1 onion
1 cup green bell pepper
1 teaspoon minced garlic
1 teaspoon almond flour
1 cup butternut squash, peeled and cubed
2 (16 oz) cans low-sodium diced tomatoes, with liquid
1 (13 oz) can baby lima beans
salt and pepper

Instructions:

Coat a large saucepan in cooking spray and place over medium heat. 2. Add chopped onion, bell pepper, and garlic and sauté until tender for about 7 minutes. Stir in the flour and cook for 1 minute. Add all the remaining ingredients and bring to a boil. Then reduce the heat and simmer for 10 to 15 minutes, or until beans are tender.

Creamy Cauliflower

⏲ 30 minutes 🍴 4 servings

Ingredients:

2 cups cauliflower florets, steamed and chopped
1/2 cup cashews
1/4 cup water
1/2 lemon juice
1 cup millet
salt

Instructions:

In a blender, add the cashews, water, lemon juice, salt, and process until smooth. Add the cauliflower and continue to process until well combined.

Slowly add in the millet and process until desired consistency.

Cloud Bread

⏲ 25 minutes 🍴 12 servings

Ingredients:

1/3 teaspoon Cream of Tartar
6 Eggs
1 cup 0% Greek Yogurt
Italian seasoning
salt

Instructions:

Preheat the oven to 300°F. Line two baking sheets with parchment paper.

Separate the egg whites and egg yolks and put the whites in a mixer with a whip attachment. Pour in the cream of tartar and beat on high until the foam turns into firm meringue peaks. Move to a separate bowl.

Add the Greek yoghurt in an empty stand mixing bowl and beat on high to soften. Add the egg yolks, one at a time, and blend. Scrape the sides of the bowl and beat until the mixture is completely smooth. Finally, add in the Italian seasoning, garlic powder, and salt.

Gently fold the firm meringue into the yolk mixture. Try to deflate the meringue as little as possible so the mixture is still firm and foamy.

Spoon 1/4 cup portions of the foam onto the baking sheets and spread into even 4-inch circles, 3/4 inch high. Make sure to leave space around each circle.

Bake in the oven for 15 to 18 minutes, or in a conventional oven for up to 30 minutes. The bread should be golden on the outside and firm. The center should not jiggle when shaken.

Cool for several minutes on the baking sheets, then move and serve!

Falafel Bites

⏰ 40 minutes 🍴 6 servings

Ingredients:

3 large eggs
2 cloves garlic
1 teaspoon ground cumin
1 teaspoon ground coriander
1 tablespoon lemon juice
1/5 cup almond flour
1/4 teaspoon sea salt
2 tablespoons coconut flour
4 cups kale

Instructions:

Preheat oven to 400°F.

Place all ingredients into a food processor. Process until a dough is formed.

Roll dough into 12 pieces and form into balls or patties. Then place into lightly oiled air fryer basket or lined cookie sheet. Bake in the preheated oven or air fry at 370°F for 18-20 minutes until golden.

Cottage Deviled Eggs

⏲ 15 minutes 🍴 2 servings

Ingredients:

8 eggs
1/2 cup 0% Greek yogurt
2 teaspoons yellow mustard
1 teaspoon coconut aminos
1/4 teaspoons garlic powder
parsley
salt and pepper

Instructions:

Hard boil the eggs and let them cool. Cut the eggs in half, remove the yolks and place the yolks in a food processor.

Add Greek yogurt, mustard, coconut aminos, garlic powder, and a pinch of salt and pepper. Process until smooth.

Transfer yolk filling into a piping bag or use a spoon to fill the egg white halves. Fill the egg halves with the yolk filling. Then dust the eggs with smokey paprika and top with parsley.

Enjoy!

Tofu Stir-Fry

⏲ 10 minutes 🍴 2 servings

Ingredients:

8 oz tofu
3 teaspoons nutritional yeast
1/4 cup onion
1/4 cup mushrooms
1 teaspoon coconut aminos
4 cups baby spinach
5 grape tomatoes
cooking spray
sriracha

Instructions:

Spray a big skillet with cooking spray and heat over medium heat. Add chopped onion and mushrooms and sauté until onions become translucent for about 2 to 3 minutes.

Add tofu to the skillet, combine and cook for another 1 to 2 minutes.

Add nutritional yeast and coconut aminos and stir until everything is combined.

Add baby spinach and grape tomatoes. Cook for 4 minutes, or until spinach starts to wilt a bit.

Serve on fresh veggies and top with sriracha or other hot sauce of your choice.

Tofu Pumpkin Curry

⏰ 30 minutes 🍴 4 servings

Ingredients:

1 tablespoon canola oil
1/2 cup onion
2 cups vegetable broth
1 can (14 oz) coconut milk
1 (15 oz) can pumpkin puree
2 teaspoons ground cumin
2 teaspoons curry powder
1 (14 oz) block of extra-firm tofu
Veggies
Salt and pepper

Instructions:

In a large pot, heat the canola oil over medium-high heat.

Add the diced onion and sauté for 3 minutes or until the onion becomes translucent.

Add water and broth, coconut milk, pumpkin puree, cumin, and curry powder, tofu, veggies of your choice, and stir well to combine.

Reduce the heat to low and let simmer for 15 minutes, stirring occasionally.

Remove from the heat. Add salt and pepper.

Fuelings

Smoothies

Unlike the ones bought in Smoothie bars or packed smoothies from groceries, these are safe to not make your insulin jump high because of the amount of sugar added. These are high protein, carb-controlled, containing wholefood ingredients that are well balanced to provide enough satiety and balanced nutrition throughout your day.

Red Velvet Smoothie

⏱ 3 minutes 🍴 2 servings

Ingredients:

2 cups almond milk
2 cups ice cubes
1/2 avocado
1/2 small boiled beetroot
3 tablespoons cocoa powder
1 scoop vanilla protein
sweetener of choice

Instructions:

Add all the ingredients to a blender and blend until completely smooth.

Add sweetener to taste.

Chocolate Protein Smoothie

⏲ 3 minutes 🍴 2 servings

Ingredients:

2 cups low-fat chocolate milk
2 tablespoons low-fat yogurt
1 banana
1 teaspoon almond butter
1 scoop protein powder (chocolate)

Instructions:

Blend all ingredients in a smoothie mixer and serve immediately.

Strawberry Cheesecake Smoothie

⏱ 3 minutes 🍴 2 servings

Ingredients:

1 cup strawberries
1 cup low-fat cottage cheese
4 oz cream cheese
1 cup ice cubes
1 cup Unsweetened Soy Milk
1 teaspoon vanilla extract
sweetener

Instructions:

Add all the ingredients to a blender and blend until completely smooth.

Add sweetener to taste.

Super-Green Smoothie

⏲ 5 minutes 🍴 2 servings

Ingredients:

2 cup unsweetened almond milk
1 frozen banana
½ cup frozen mango
2 handfuls baby spinach
¼ cup pumpkin seeds
2 tablespoons hemp seeds
1 scoop vanilla protein powder
½ cup water
Sweetener (optional)

Instructions:

Add all the ingredients to a blender and blend until completely smooth.

Add sweetener if desired.

Piña-Colada Smoothie

5 minutes | 2 servings

Ingredients:

2 cups unsweetened coconut milk
2 cups pineapple
1 banana
1/2 cup orange juice
1 cup Greek yogurt
1 cup ice

Instructions:

Add all the ingredients to a blender and blend until completely smooth.

Su-Pear Smoothie

5 minutes   2 servings

Ingredients:

2 small pears
1 frozen banana
1 scoop vanilla protein powder
1 teaspoon cinnamon
1 teaspoon cardamon
1 cup almond milk
1 cup ice

Instructions:

Add all ingredients to a blender and process until smooth.

Lemon Poppy Smoothie

⏲ 5 minutes 🍴 2 servings

Ingredients:

2 teaspoons poppy seeds
3 tablespoons lemon juice
1 tablespoon grated lemon zest
1 cup low-fat yogurt
2 tablespoons chicory syrup
½ cup water (or more)
½ cup ice

Instructions:

Add all ingredients to a blender and process until smooth.

Orange Smoothie

⏲ 5 minutes 🍴 2 servings

Ingredients:

2 medium oranges
1 frozen banana
1/2 cup Greek yogurt
1 scoop vanilla protein powder
1 cup ice cubes
Sweetener

Instructions:

In a blender, process oranges, then add banana and the remaining ingredients except for the sweetener. Blend until smooth. Sweeten to taste or add water, if needed.

Serve immediately.

Filling Raspberry Smoothie

⏲ 5 minutes 🍴 2 servings

Ingredients:

1 medium avocado
3/4 cup raspberries
1 scoop protein powder
1 tablespoon lemon juice
1 ½ cup unsweetened coconut milk

Instructions:

Add all the ingredients to a blender and blend until completely smooth.

Salted Caramel Potion

⏲ 5 minutes 🍴 2 servings

Ingredients:

1 scoop protein powder (Salted Caramel flavor)
1/3 cup mashed sweet potato
2 dates
1 tablespoon almond butter
1 cup almond milk
salt
1 cup ice

Instructions:

Add all the ingredients to a blender and blend until completely smooth.

Enjoy your potion!

Protein Bars

Protein Bars are a perfect grab-and-go snack and an excellent alternative for the raffinate, overpriced bars that you can buy in shops or online. You can create these easily at home, you know the ingredients you use, and their final price is far below the branded ones. You can store them in your fridge safely for about a week or in your freezer. Swap the purchased sweets for these healthy and filling protein bars and feed your body with the right nutrients!

Coffee Protein Bars

⏲ 20 minutes 🍴 10 servings

Ingredients:

1 cup hazelnuts
1 teaspoon ground coffee
2 scoops protein powder
2/3 cups hazelnut butter
3 tablespoons chicory syrup (or honey)
2 tablespoons coconut oil
1/2 teaspoon vanilla extract
sea salt

Instructions:

Using a mixer, grind nuts until they are coarse, then transfer to a medium bowl.

Add all the remaining ingredients, stirring well to combine.

Press into a lined baking dish and refrigerate until firm.

Slice into bars and enjoy.

Vanilla Nougat Protein Bars

⏲ 10 minutes 🍴 12 servings

Ingredients:

½ cup chicory syrup
4 scoops protein powder
2 teaspoons vanilla extract
1 tablespoon flaked almonds
1 tablespoon coconut oil

Instructions:

Heat chicory syrup in a medium bowl in the microwave for about half a minute, until you see it starts to bubble. Add all ingredients and stir.

With your hands, mix the ingredients until it starts to form a sticky but dry consistency.

Press into molds of choice or slice tray.

Cinnamon Roll Protein Bars

⏱ 20 minutes 🍴 10 servings

Ingredients:

½ cup coconut flour
1 cup smooth cashew butter
¼ cup chicory syrup
1 tablespoon cinnamon
4 oz cream cheese
¼ cup erythritol

Instructions:

Line a square pan with parchment paper and set aside.

Add coconut flour into a big bowl and combine with cashew butter, chicory syrup, and cinnamon. Mix until you get a thick batter. If the batter is too thick to work with, add water. If it's too thin, add more flour.

Put the batter into the lined pan and let it sit in the refrigerator for few minutes.

In another bowl, mix the softened cream cheese with half a tablespoon of cinnamon and your sweetener. Spread the frosting over the chilled cinnamon roll bar base.

Once firm, cut into 12 bars and enjoy!

Pepperoat Bars

⏲ 10 minutes +freezing 🍴 12 servings

Ingredients:

2 2/3 cups rolled oats
1 cup almonds
0.67 cup dried cranberries
1/3 cup pumpkin seeds
1/3 teaspoon black pepper
2/3 cup almond butter
1/3 cup chicory syrup (or honey)

Instructions:

In a large bowl, combine oats, almonds, cranberries, pumpkin seeds, and black pepper.

In a microwave-safe bowl, combine almond butter and honey, then microwave for 30 seconds, or until hot and pourable.

Gently combine hot almond butter mix with the dry oat mix.

Line a 9x13 inch sheet with parchment paper and sprinkle in the granola mixture. Press firmly with a spatula or your hand so that the granola is compact.

Put the sheet in the freezer for 15 to 30 minutes to firm up, then cut into 12 bars.

Noat-Bake Protein Bars

⏰ 5 minutes 🍴 12 servings

Ingredients:

1/2 cups ground oats
1 cup chia seeds
2 scoops vanilla protein powder
1/2 cup smooth almond butter Can use any nut or seed butter

2 tablespoons chicory syrup
2 teaspoons chocolate chips
water if needed

Instructions:

Line a 10 x 10-inch pan with parchment paper and set aside.

In a large mixing bowl, add chia seeds, ground oats, and the protein powder, mix and set aside.

In a microwave-safe bowl, mix almond butter with chicory syrup and melt until well combined. Add the wet mixture into the dry mixture and mix until fully incorporated. Add 1 or 2 teaspoons of water, if needed, to form a thick batter. Be careful not to add too much.

Pour the batter into the lined pan and press firmly in place.

Finally, drizzle chocolate chips on the top, refrigerate until firm, then cut into 12 bars.

Pumpkin Protein Bars

⏲ 25 minutes 🍴 10 servings

Ingredients:

1 (15 oz) can white beans
1/2 cup pumpkin purée
4 tablespoons maple syrup
1 teaspoon pumpkin pie spice
1/4 teaspoon salt
1 cup pumpkin spice Cheerios
6 scoops protein powder (vanilla)
1 1/2 cups old-fashioned oats
1 cup almond flour

Instructions:

Preheat oven to 350°F.

Add Oats and cheerios into a food processor and blend until smooth, add protein and almond flour and mix shortly. Then pour in wet ingredients and mix until smooth.

Lightly spray a baking dish with a cooking spray and spread the mixture out evenly.

Place in oven and bake for 15 – 18 minutes, or until set. Remove and cut into 10 bars.

No-Bake Nana-Cake Bars

⏲ 15 minutes + refrigerate 🍴 10 servings

Ingredients:

2 cups oat flour
½ cup coconut flour
½ cup vanilla protein powder
2 tablespoons erythritol
1 tablespoons cinnamon
1/4 cup nut butter
½ cup chicory syrup
1 banana
1/4 cup chopped nuts
1 tablespoon + water

Instructions:

Line a large baking sheet with parchment paper.

In a large bowl, combine the flours, protein powder, erythritol, and cinnamon.

In a microwave-safe bowl, melt the nut butter and chicory syrup and combine.

Pour the wet mixture into the dry mix. Add the mashed banana and stir well until combined.

Add a teaspoon or tablespoon of water, or more, if needed, until you get a thick and firm batter. The consistency will depend on the protein powder and flour brand you use.

Then, put on the lined baking dish and press firmly onto it. Refrigerate for at least 30 minutes and cut into squares or bars.

Peanut Butter Bomb

⏱ 15 minutes 🍴 40 servings

Ingredients:

2 cups smooth peanut butter
1/2 cup chicory syrup (or honey)
3/4 cup coconut flour

Instructions:

Line a baking sheet with parchment paper and put it aside.

Put all the ingredients in a big bowl and combine thoroughly. If the batter is too thick, add drops of water carefully until you get a thick batter that you can form.

With your hands, form the dough into small balls and place it on the lined sheet. The number of bombs will depend on the size you'll create.

Refrigerate the bombs balls for 30 minutes or overnight.

No-Bake Coconut Bars

⏱ 10 minutes 🍴 20 servings

Ingredients:

3 cups coconut flakes
1 cup coconut oil
¼ cup chicory syrup

Instructions:

Line a baking sheet with parchment paper and put it aside.

Put the shredded coconut into a large mixing bowl. Melt coconut oil and add it to the coconut together with the syrup. Mix well until you get a thick batter. If it is too thick, carefully add a few drops of water.

Pour the mixture into the pan or sheet. With your wet hands, press the mixture firmly into the lined pan. Before refrigerating, cut into bars.

Refrigerate or freeze until firm.

Dark Chocolate & Sea Salt Bars

⏲ 15 minutes 🍴 20 servings

Ingredients:

5 oz almonds
5 oz cashews
16 oz pitted dried dates
1 1/4 cups egg white protein powder
1/2 cup unsweetened cocoa powder
1/2 teaspoon sea salt

Instructions:

Line the sheet with parchment paper.

Add the almonds and cashews to a food processor and process until finely chopped.

Add the egg white protein and cocoa powder and process. Add the dates and process for another 2 minutes until a slightly tacky dough forms. It should hold together when pressed.

With your fingers, press the mixture into the lined sheet. Sprinkle with the salt and press lightly to adhere.

Before refrigerating, cut into bars. Refrigerate for at least 1 hour or overnight or freeze for 30 minutes.

You can store the bars in an air-tight container. You can divide them with a piece of parchment paper or wrap each bar individually.

Desserts

Berry Cheesecake Muffins

⏲ 40 minutes 🍴 12 servings

Ingredients:

1 cup fat-free Greek yogurt
2 tablespoons fat-free cottage cheese
1 tablespoon coconut flour
1/4 cup dried berries
2 eggs
6 scoops protein powder (vanilla)
1 cup fresh blackberries

Instructions:

Preheat the oven to 340°F.

Spray a 12 cup muffin pan with a cooking spray. Place all ingredients except the blackberries in a food processor or blender and process until well combined. Move to a large mixing bowl, add the blackberries, and gently fold in.

Pour the batter evenly into the muffin pan, only filling each cup to 3/4 full. Put the muffins in the oven and bake for 35 minutes, or until a toothpick inserted into the middle comes out clean.

Mouse Dessert

⏰ 5 minutes + refrigerate 🍴 2 servings

Ingredients:

20 g cocoa
30 g chocolate protein powder
1 cup sugar-free gelatin
2 tablespoon light cream cheese
4 tablespoons cold water
1/2 cup crushed ice

Instructions:

Place all ingredients in a blender. Pulse until smooth.

Pour into glass and place in the fridge to set.

Serve chilled.

Protein Chia Pudding

⏲ 2 minutes + overnight 🍴 1 serving

Ingredients:

1 cup unsweetened almond milk
2 tablespoons chia seeds
1/2 scoop protein powder

Instructions:

Mix protein powder in the almond milk very well and add in the chia seeds. You can exchange the protein powder with cocoa powder or cinnamon if you want to experiment.

Pour in a glass jar, cover, and let it sit in the refrigerator overnight, so it thickens.

Serve with fresh or frozen berries.

Double Chocolate Protein Fudge

⏲ 30 minutes + freeze 🍴 12 servings

Ingredients:

½ cup almonds
2 tablespoons oats
1 cup chocolate protein powder
¼ cup cocoa powder
½ cup pitted dates
½ cup dried figs
2 tablespoons almond butter
¼ cup unsweetened almond milk

Instructions:

In a mixer, mix the dates, figs, almond butter, protein powder, cocoa powder, and almond milk until you get a sticky consistency.

Add the almonds and oats and process again. You might leave chunks of non-processed pieces in the batter if you like.

Line a 8 x 8 baking pan with parchment paper and fill with the fudge mixture.

Using a spatula, smooth the fudge in the pan and top with another piece of parchment paper and press down to make sure the fudge is pressed in an even layer.

Place the fudge in the freezer for at least 1 hour. Once set, remove the parchment from the pan and cut it on a cutting board into 12 bars.

Store in the fridge or freezer.

Energy Bites

⏲ 10 minutes 🍴 20 servings

Ingredients:

1 cup smooth peanut butter
½ cup coconut flour
3 tablespoons chicory syrup

Instructions:

Line a baking sheet with parchment paper and put it aside.

In a bowl, add the peanut butter, coconut flour, and chicory syrup.

Mix until smooth. Use a silicone spatula to fold until well combined and thickened.

Using a cookie scoop, scoop and drop peanut butter balls on the prepared baking sheet.

Store in an air-tight container in the refrigerator for up to two weeks.

Enjoy!

Protein Oreos

⏱ 50 minutes 🍴 6 servings

Ingredients:

Cookies:
1 tablespoon Coconut Flour
1/2 cup Liquid Egg Whites
1/4 cup Whey Protein Powder
2 tablespoons Cocoa Powder
1 tablespoon Cocoa Nibs
1/8 cup Rolled Oats
1 teaspoon Baking Powder
Filling:
1/8 cup vanilla protein powder
1/4 cup Water
1 teaspoon Coconut Flour

Instructions:

Blend the cookie ingredients, form 6 cookies on a cookie tray and bake at 338°F for about 25 minutes.

The cookies are ready when a wooden stick comes out clean. Let them cool and cut each piece lengthwise into three (you can cut the top part smaller and leave it aside, you can crush it on top of your yogurt another day). You will end up with 12 cookie halves for your Oreos.

Place them on the cookie tray again and let them bake for another five minutes. If they are already dry, you can skip this step.

For the filling, mix 1/8 cup of protein powder, 1/4 cup of water, and a teaspoon of coconut flour.

Spread the filling on one cookie half and top it with another cookie.

Serve with milk or any way you're used to eat your Oreos.

Chickpea Cookie Dough

⏲ 10 minutes + refrigerate 🍴 4 servings

Ingredients:

5 scoops Vegan Protein
1 can chickpeas
2 tablespoons almond butter
½ cup almond milk
½ cup Greek yogurt
¾ teaspoon vanilla extract
1 banana
1 teaspoon cinnamon
Dark chocolate, cacao nibs, mixed nuts, and dried fruit

Instructions:

Rinse and clean the chickpeas very well in cold water. Get rid of as much of the thin outer shells as possible, which improves the texture and consistency.

Once the chickpeas are clean, put them in a mixer with almond milk and blend until smooth.

Add two heaped tablespoons of almond butter, Greek yogurt, vanilla extract, banana or banana baby food, and cinnamon and blend well until the mixture is very smooth, scraping down the sides if necessary.

Add in the additions of choice such ad dark chocolate chips, cacao nibs, mixed nuts, or dried fruit and store in the fridge for a while before serving.

Molten Chocolate Mug Cake

⏲ 2 minutes 🍴 1 serving

Ingredients:

1 banana
1 egg
1 scoop chocolate protein
1 tablespoon cacao powder
½ teaspoon baking powder
1 square dark chocolate

Instructions:

In a microwave-safe bowl, combine mashed banana, egg, protein powder, cacao powder, baking powder, and if desired, add up to a teaspoon of a sweetener.

Stick the square of dark chocolate in the center of the bowl and your mixture for the melting center.

Microwave for about 1 and a half minute and serve immediately.

Tiramisu Protein Pancakes

⏱ 10 minutes 🍴 2 servings

Ingredients:

Pancakes:
1 cup coconut flour
1 scoop protein powder (vanilla or cappuccino)
1 teaspoon baking powder
1 tablespoon greek yogurt
2 tablespoons cold-brewed coffee
10 drops stevia
2 Egg Whites
Filling:
1 cup cottage cheese
1 teaspoon rum (extract)
2 teaspoons granulated sweetener

Instructions:

Mix all ingredients for the pancakes.

In a pan, heat the coconut oil and make about 8 to 10 pancakes.

In a high bowl, mix the cream's ingredients with a hand blender to get rid of the lumps.

Stack the pancakes and layer with the cream and serve dusted with some cocoa on top and sugar-free syrup (chocolate or coffee flavor).

Enjoy!

Protein Peanut Butter Cups

1 hour 20 minutes 12 servings

Ingredients:

1 cup chocolate chips
1 tablespoon coconut oil
3 tablespoons smooth peanut butter
3 tablespoons protein powder

Instructions:

Line a muffin pan with 12 muffin cups.

In a microwave-safe cup, put the chocolate chips and coconut oil, microwave for 30-second intervals until melted, and mix each time until smooth.

Then, pour a thin layer of the melted chocolate on the bottom of each cup and place the pan into the freezer for 10 minutes.

In a bowl, combine peanut butter and protein powder of your choice. I have used vanilla. Roll the batter with your hands into teaspoon-sized balls.

Put one ball in each cup and press on the chocolate layer, leaving a little rim around the edges, where you will pour the remaining chocolate.

Cover and put in the fridge for at least half an hour. Take them out a few minutes before serving to melt slightly.

Soups

As well as for the previous fuelings, you don't need to buy packed, expensive soups. You can make your own at home and have double the amount with the same (or lower) budget, know exactly what's the soup made of and what you put into your body. You can cook more in advance and have it ready in your fridge for a few days upfront.

Broccoli-Parmesan Chicken Soup

⏲ 45 minutes 🍴 4 servings

Ingredients:

20 oz shredded chicken
32 oz broccoli
4 cups chicken broth
2 tablespoons olive oil
2 cloves garlic
1 onion

3 cups baby spinach
1/2 cup Parmesan
1 tablespoon lemon zest
3 tablespoons lemon juice
Salt and Pepper

Instructions:

Cut the broccoli into small florets and slice the stems.

In a large pot, heat the olive oil on medium heat and add garlic and onion. Cook for about 2 minutes. Add chopped broccoli stems, flavor with salt and pepper, and let it cook covered for about 3 other minutes.

Add broccoli florets and 1/2 cup water, cover, and let it steam up to 6 minutes. Remove half of the florets to a separate bowl and set aside.

Add chicken broth and baby spinach and let it simmer for 10 minutes. In the end, add grated parmesan, lemon zest, and lemon juice, and mix with a hand blender.

To the smooth soup, pop in the shredded chicken and left broccoli florets.

Vegan Broccoli Cheddar Soup

⏲ 25 minutes 🍴 2 servings

Ingredients:

2 cups chicken broth
3 cups broccoli
4 Laughing Cow cheese wedges
1 cup cheddar cheese
garlic powder
Salt and pepper

Instructions:

Add the chicken broth into a medium pot, add chopped broccoli, 1/8 teaspoon salt, 1/8 teaspoon of pepper, and 1/8 teaspoon of garlic powder. Bring to a boil, then reduce to a simmer for 12 to 15 minutes.

Add the cheese wedges and stir until melted down. Then, pour the soup into a mixer and blend until evenly mixed. Pour into two bowls and sprinkle each bowl with ¼ cup cheddar cheese.

White Chicken Chili

⏲ 30 minutes 🍴 4 servings

Ingredients:

1 tablespoon olive oil
1 medium onion
3 cloves garlic
1 jalapeno
30 oz white beans
4 oz green chiles
4 cups chicken broth
1 lime

1 teaspoon ground cumin
½ teaspoon chili powder
¼ teaspoon dried oregano
2 cups rotisserie chicken
⅓ cup cilantro
Salt and black pepper
avocado slices, shredded cheese, sour cream, cilantro

Instructions:

Heat the oil over medium heat in a big pot. Cook the onion until it becomes translucent for about 3 to 4 minutes, then add the diced garlic and jalapeno and cook for 2 more minutes.

Add the rinsed and drained white beans, diced green chiles, chicken broth, the juice from 1 lime, ground cumin, chili powder, oregano, shredded chicken, cilantro, salt, and pepper. Mix everything and let it simmer on low heat for about 15 minutes.

Ladle the soup into bowls and serve with toppings of your choice: avocado slices, shredded cheese, sour cream, or a combination of all and top it off with cilantro.

Enjoy!

Tomato Soup

⏰ 45 minutes 🍴 4 servings

Ingredients:

4 tablespoons butter
1/2 large onion
1 (28 oz) can tomatoes
1 1/2 cups water
salt

Instructions:

In a large saucepan, melt the butter over medium heat.

Add onion cut to wedges, water, can of tomatoes with the juice or about 10 medium tomatoes instead, and about a half teaspoon of salt. Bring to a boil and cook uncovered for about 40 minutes.

Stir occasionally and add more salt to taste.

Blend the soup with a hand mixer, and season more if desired.

Sprinkle with chopped fresh basil and shredded mozzarella on top for the serving. Enjoy!

Pea and Ham Soup

⏲ 12 minutes 🍴 4 servings

Ingredients:

1/8 cup butter
6 spring onions
18 oz frozen petit pois
2 ½ cups vegetable or chicken broth
10 oz chicken ham

Instructions:

In a saucepan, melt the butter and cook the spring onions for 5 minutes until softened.

Add the peas and broth and bring back to a simmer, then cook for 3 minutes.

Mix in a small handful of the chopped ham, simmer for 2 minutes, remove from the heat and use a hand blender to mix everything.

Season, stir in the rest of the Try ham, then serve.

Cauliflower Soup

⏲ 30 minutes 🍴 8 servings

Ingredients:

1 medium cauliflower
1 carrot
1/4 cup celery
2 1/2 cups water
2 teaspoons chicken bouillon
3 tablespoons butter
2 tablespoons all-purpose flour
2 cups milk
1 cup cheddar cheese
1 teaspoon hot sauce
Salt and pepper

Instructions:

Add the cauliflower florets, shredded carrot, chopped celery, water, and bouillon and bring to a boil in a big pot. Reduce the heat and let it simmer covered for about 15 minutes until vegetables are tender.

Melt butter in a big saucepan. Add the flour, a tiny bit of salt and pepper to taste and whisk well until smooth. Slowly add milk, stirring constantly.

Bring it to a boil over medium heat and let it cook, continually stirring for 2 minutes, until it thickens. Reduce the heat, add the shredded cheese, and let it melt at this point, or sprinkle on top when serving. Add hot pepper sauce if you like. Then, stir the mixture from the saucepan into the cauliflower mixture.

Stir and cook one more minute and serve.

Cheesy Ham Chowder

⏲ 30 minutes 🍴 10 servings

Ingredients:

10 bacon strips
1 large onion
1 cup carrots
3 tablespoons all-purpose flour
3 cups milk
1 1/2 cups water
2 1/2 cups potatoes
1 can (15 oz) whole kernel corn
2 teaspoons chicken bouillon
3 cups cheddar cheese
2 cups ham
Pepper

Instructions:

In a big pot, cook the bacon over medium heat until crisp. Then remove bacon with a slotted spoon to a paper towel to drain.

In the bacon fat, sauté onion and carrots for a few minutes. Stir in flour until blended. Slowly add milk and water and bring to a boil. Cook until thickened for about 2 more minutes.

Add cubed potatoes, drained corn, bouillon, and pepper. Reduce the heat and let it simmer uncovered, for about 20 minutes, until the potatoes become tender.

Add shredded cheese and ham and heat until the cheese is melted. Lastly, stir in the bacon.

Serve and enjoy!

Potato Soup

⏲ 30 minutes 🍴 8 servings

Ingredients:

6 bacon strips
3 cups potatoes
1 small carrot
1/2 cup onion
1 tablespoon parsley
1/2 teaspoon celery seed
1 can (14 oz) chicken broth
3 tablespoons all-purpose flour
3 cups milk
8 oz mozzarella
2 green onions
Salt and pepper

Instructions:

In a big saucepan, cook diced bacon strips over medium heat until crisp. Drain the drippings and add vegetables, seasonings, and broth and bring to a boil.

Reduce heat slightly and let it simmer covered for about 15 minutes until the potatoes are tender.

Mix the flour and milk until smooth and stir into the soup. Bring to a boil and let it cook until thickened, about 2 minutes, stirring constantly. Add shredded mozzarella and stir until melted.

Serve with green onions or skip this step if desired.

Crab Soup

⏲ 20 minutes 🍴 4 servings

Ingredients:

16 oz crab meat
3 tablespoons butter
1 cup heavy whipping cream
3 cups milk
1 tablespoon cooking sherry
Salt and pepper

Instructions:

In a big saucepan, melt the butter. Add the crab meat, whipping cream, and milk and bring to a boil over medium heat. Reduce the heat and let it simmer for about 20 minutes.

Remove from the heat and add the cooking sherry and salt and pepper to taste.

Serve with lemon wedges and saltine crackers.

Corn Chowder

⏲ 60 minutes 🍴 10 servings

Ingredients:

2 tablespoons butter
3 cloves garlic
1 large sweet onion
2 teaspoons smoked paprika
1 ½ teaspoon dry thyme
½ cup dry white wine

6 cups chicken broth
3 stalks celery
2 large potatoes
4 ½ cups corn
2/3 cup heavy cream
Salt and pepper

Instructions:

In a large pot, melt butter over medium heat. Then add minced garlic and chopped onion. Stir and cook for about 4 minutes until the onions start to brown.

Add smoked paprika, thyme, salt, and pepper and stir for about 30 seconds, until the spices are fragrant. Then add white wine to prevent the spices from scorching. Let it cook for about 1 minute or until the wine has mostly evaporated.

Add in broth, chopped celery, cubed, peeled potatoes, and corn. Bring it to a boil and cook for 20 minutes until the potatoes are soft, then remove from the heat.

Take 3 cups of the soup from the pot and set aside. Place the rest of the soup in a blender and blend until smooth, then pour in the non-mixed soup into the pureed soup. Finally, add in the heavy cream and stir everything.

You can serve it topped with chopped, crispy bacon and scallions, sour cream, sprinkled with chipotle powder.

Enjoy!

Quick Snack Tips

Quick snack tips to grab anywhere on the go if you forgot to meal prep, you don't want to grab a random fast food, and you still want to stick to the healthy choices. You can prepare some of the recipes from this category in advance, keep them in your freezer and grab them anytime you'll be running out of time. In both cases, there's no need to dismiss healthy alternatives. Be ready, and you won't need to make up any excuses!

Celery and Peanut Butter

⏲ 5 minutes 🍴 4 servings

Ingredients:

4 celery stalks
4 tablespoons peanut butter

Instructions:

Cut the celery stalks and cut them through in two halves.

Spread peanut butter onto the celery or serve it on the side for dipping.

You can replace the celery with a carrot, cucumber, or an apple. It's a healthy and extremely easy snack. You can cut more celery sticks in advance and keep them in an air-tight container in your fridge.

Poppy Crackers

⏰ 30 minutes 🍴 20 servings

Ingredients:

1 ½ cups almond flour
1 tablespoon poppy seeds
1 tablespoon olive oil
1 teaspoon Himalayan salt
1 egg white

Instructions:

Preheat the oven to 350°F and put the rack in the middle. Line a baking sheet with parchment paper and set aside.

In a large bowl, mix almond flour, poppy seeds, olive oil, egg white, and salt.

Pour the mixture over a lined baking sheet, cover with a parchment paper sheet, and roll out the dough to a thin rectangle with a rolling pin. Carefully take off the top parchment paper and cut into crackers using a pizza cutter or a knife.

Bake for about 15 minutes until golden brown. Watch closely for the last 5 minutes, as every oven might bake slightly differently, so you won't burn your crackers. Remove from the oven and let cool completely.

Once cool, carefully snap the crackers apart along the score line.

Store at room temperature in a container with a tight-fitting lid. You can store this for about a week.

Frozen Yogurt Blueberries

⏲ 5 minutes + freezing 🍴 4 servings

Ingredients:

2 cups low-fat Greek yogurt
2 teaspoons chicory syrup (or honey)
4 cups blueberries
½ cup pistachios

Instructions:

Line a freezer-safe container with parchment paper.

In a big bowl, mix well yogurt and honey. Dip the blueberries in the yogurt mixture.

Place in a parchment-lined container, making sure they are not touching, and sprinkle them with chopped pistachios.

Let it freeze until yogurt is set. Store in an air-tight container in the freezer until serving.

Apple Muffins

⏲ 45 minutes 🍴 18 servings

Ingredients:

2 cups coconut flour
1/2 cup coconut sugar
1 teaspoon baking soda
1/2 teaspoon baking powder
1/2 teaspoon salt
1 teaspoon cinnamon
1 teaspoon flaxseed
1 teaspoon vanilla extract
1/2 cup coconut oil
3 apples
1/4 cup xylitol
1 teaspoon cinnamon

Instructions:

Preheat the oven to 350 °F.

Grind flax seeds and mix them with 2 ½ tablespoons of water to create a flax egg mixture and let it sit for a few minutes.

Mix all dry ingredients, then add in all wet ingredients. Chop up the apples into small pieces and add them to the mix. Add the flax egg and mix well.

Scoop the final mixture into a muffin tin or baking cups. Mix xylitol as an alternative for sugar and cinnamon and sprinkle over the muffins.

Bake in the oven for 20 minutes.

Enjoy!

Sweet Potato Chips

⏱ 1 hour 30 minutes 🍴 4 servings

Ingredients:

1 sweet potato
1 tablespoon olive oil
1/2 teaspoon curry powder
salt

Instructions:

Preheat oven to 275°F.

Scrub the potatoes, remove blemishes, and pat dry. Slice the potatoes into round pieces.

In a big bowl, mix the potato slices and coat them with the olive oil.

Line a cookie sheet with foil and fill the sheet placing the chips next to each other. Bake for 40 minutes, then turn the potatoes over and bake for another 40 minutes, or more, until the edges are crispy.

You might need to use two sheets. In that case, place the sheets in the middle and bottom rack and switch them after the first 40 minutes, when you will turn your chips.

Sprinkle with curry powder or other preferred spices.

Let the potatoes cool at room temperature. They will become crispier. Store in an air-tight container. Remember, these are not artificial, so they need to be consumed within 3 to 4 days.

Breakfast Sandwiches

⏲ 30 minutes 🍴 6 servings

Ingredients:

6 large eggs
6 English muffins
12 slices ham
6 slices cheddar cheese
Salt and pepper

Instructions:

Preheat oven to 375°F. Lightly spray six 10 oz ramekins with cooking spray and place onto a baking sheet.

Add one beaten egg to each ramekin and season it with salt and pepper. Place in the oven and bake until egg whites are cooked for about 12 to 14 minutes.

Layer one egg on a muffin bottom. Top with two ham slices and one slice cheddar, and another muffin top. Repeat with remaining English muffins to make six sandwiches.

Wrap each sandwich tightly in a plastic wrap and put it in the freezer.

Before serving, remove the plastic wrap and wrap it in a paper towel. Warm in the microwave for 1 to 2 minutes.

Serve and enjoy your quick breakfast!

Beef and Cheddar Roll-Ups

⏱ 5 minutes 🍴 1 serving

Ingredients:

1 slice roast beef
½ slice cheddar cheese
1 teaspoon Thousand Island Yogurt Dressing
onion
tomato

Instructions:

Adjust your ingredients up to how many rolls you want to prep.

Layer the thinly sliced roast beef with cheddar cheese, dressing, and veggies.

Roll up, cut in half if desired, and serve.

Skinny Burrito in a Jar

⏲ 15 minutes 🍴 4 servings

Ingredients:

1 cup salsa
15 oz black beans
1 cup cheddar cheese
1/2 cup Greek yogurt

Instructions:

Layer each ingredient into 4 canning jars. Start with 1/4 cup salsa, 1/4 heaping cup of drained black beans, 1/4 cup shredded cheese, and 2 tablespoons of yogurt (or sour cream).

Refrigerate for up to two days.

Overnight Oats

⏲ 5 minutes 🍴 4 servings

Ingredients:

2 cups old-fashioned rolled oats
2 cups milk
1 cup plain Greek yogurt
3 tablespoons honey
1 tablespoon chia seeds
1/4 teaspoon cinnamon
1/4 teaspoon salt
toppings

Instructions:

Put all the ingredients into a large bowl and stir together until combined.

Divide the oats into 4 jars or adjust the amount if needed. Cover and refrigerate overnight.

Add toppings of your choice: fresh berries, nuts, seeds, nut butter, or zero-sugar syrup.

Roasted Chickpeas

⏲ 45 minutes 🍴 3 servings

Ingredients:

15 oz chickpeas
olive oil
1/8 teaspoon kosher salt
1/4 teaspoon chili powder
1/4 teaspoon ground cumin
1/4 teaspoon paprika
1/4 teaspoon ground coriander
1/4 teaspoon curry powder
1/4 teaspoon garlic powder

Instructions:

Preheat oven to 375°F.

Drain and rinse your chickpeas and let them dry completely with a paper towel if needed.

Place the chickpeas on a baking sheet in a single layer and roast in the oven for about 30 to 45 minutes, mixing every few minutes. The chickpeas will become golden brown and crunchy but check on them so they won't burn.

In a bowl, combine the spices. Remove chickpeas from the oven and spray with olive oil. Then toss the spices immediately on while hot.

Let it cool slightly and eat.

Shopping List

0% Greek yogurt
all-purpose flour
all-purpose seasoning
almond butter (smooth)
almond flour
almond milk (unsweetened)
almonds
apples
asparagus
assorted microgreens
avocado
avocado oil
baby gem lettuce
baby lima beans (13 oz) can
baby spinach
bacon strips
Baking Powder
baking soda
balsamic vinegar
banana
barbecue sauce
bass fillets
beef Ribeye Steak
bell pepper
big red peppers
black beans (14 oz) can
black pepper
blueberries
broccoli
Brussels sprouts
butter
butternut squash
cabbage
cacao powder
canola oil
cardamon
carrot
cashews
cauliflower
cayenne pepper
celery
cilantro
cinnamon
coarsely chopped fresh mango
cocoa
Cocoa Nibs
cocoa powder
cocoa powder (unsweetened)
coconut aminos
coconut cream
coconut flakes
coconut flour
coconut milk (14 oz) can
coconut milk (unsweetened)
coconut oil
Cod Fillets
coffee
coley
cooking sherry
Cooking spray
corn
corn starch
arrowroot
cottage cheese
crab meat
cranberries
cream cheese
Cream of Tartar
cucumber
Cumin
curry powder
Dark chocolate
dates
Dijon mustard
dried cranberries
dried figs
dried oregano
Dried Parsley
dried thyme
dry white wine
Egg white protein powder
eggs
English muffins
erythritol
extra virgin olive oil
extra-firm tofu (14 oz) block
fajita seasoning
fat-free cottage cheese
finely riced cauliflower
flaked almonds
flank steaks
flax seed
fresh basil leaves
fresh blackberries
fresh coriander
fresh dill
fresh chives
fresh mint leaves
fresh pineapple
fresh red chilies
fresh rosemary
fresh strawberries
fresh thyme
freshly grated horseradish
fruity olive oil
garam masala
garlic
garlic powder
Ghee
ginger
ginger paste
grape tomatoes
green bell pepper
green chiles
green onions
green pesto
ground cumin
ground beef
ground cayenne pepper
ground coriander
ground cumin
ground fennel
ground ginger
ground mustard seeds
halibut fillets
halibut steaks
hazelnuts
heavy whipping cream
hemp seeds
Himalayan salt
honey
hot red pepper sauce
cheddar cheese
cherry tomatoes
chia seeds
chicken bouillon
chicken breast
chicken broth (14 oz) can
chicken drumsticks
chicken ham
chicken stock cubes
chicken wings
chickpeas (15 oz) can
chicory syrup
chili garlic sauce
Chili Powder

Chinese five-spice powder
chocolate chips
chopped fresh basil
Italian seasoning
jalapeno
Kalamata olives
kale
kiwi
Laughing Cow cheese wedges
lemon
lettuce
light cream cheese
light mayonnaise
lime
Liquid Egg Whites
low-fat cottage cheese
low-fat feta cheese
low-fat chocolate milk
low-sodium diced tomatoes (16 oz) can
mahi mahi fillets
mango
mango chutney
maple syrup
marinated seitan pieces
mayonnaise
milk
millet
minced garlic
mint leaves
mozzarella
mushrooms
mustard
nutritional yeast
oat flour
oats
old-fashioned oats
onion
onion powder
orange
oregano
oregano leaves
pak choi
paprika
Parmesan
parsley
peanut butter
peanut butter (smooth)
peanuts
pears
pepper
petit pois
pineapple
pistachios
pitted dried dates

poppy seeds
pork loin
pork shoulder roast
pork tenderloin
potatoes
protein powder (Cappuccino)
protein powder (Chocolate)
protein powder (Salted Caramel)
protein powder (Vanilla)
protein powder (vegan)
pumpkin
pumpkin pie spice
pumpkin puree (15 oz) can
pumpkin seeds
pumpkin spice Cheerios
raisin bran cereal
raspberries
red bell pepper
red chili
red kidney beans (15 oz) can
red onion
red pepper
Red pepper flakes
red wine vinegar
rice vinegar
roast beef
roasted turkey meat
rolled oats
Romaine salad
rotisserie chicken
rum (extract)
salmon filets
salsa
scallions
serrano chiles
sesame oil
sesame seeds
shallots
shirataki mushrooms
shirataki noodles
shoulder steak
shredded cheese, sour cream, cilantro
shredded chicken
shrimps
skirt steak
smoked paprika
smooth cashew butter
smooth peanut butter
snap peas
snipped fresh cilantro

snow peas
sour cream
soy sauce
spelt flour
spinach
sprigs fresh rosemary
sprigs fresh thyme
spring onions
square dark chocolate
sriracha
steak
steak seasoning blend
stevia
strawberries
sugar snap peas
sweet paprika
sweet potato
sweetener
tamari sauce
teriyaki sauce
Thousand Island Yogurt Dressing
tilapia fillets
tofu
tomato paste
tomato purée
tomatoes
tomatoes (14 oz) can
tomatoes (28 oz) can
tuna (5 oz) can
tuna fillets
turkey breast
turkey ham
turmeric
unsweetened almond milk
unsweetened coconut milk
unsweetened Soy Milk
vanilla extract
vegetable broth
vegetable oil
white beans (15 oz) can
White Pepper
whole grain bread crumbles
whole grain flour
whole kernel corn (15 oz) can
Wild Salmon Fillets
xylitol
yellow bell pepper
yellow mustard
yellow plantains
zucchini

Conclusion

I hope this book will help you on your journey to losing weight while keeping the weight-loss sustainable. Providing a wide variety of meals, healthy alternatives of snacks, and homemade swaps of fuelings, your diet will be more flexible, more complex, whole food, nutrient-dense, and still amazingly delicious.

With this cookbook, the diet plan will not be a diet anymore but will become a lifestyle and much more comfortable.

If you have enjoyed this book, please leave me a review on Amazon.
For me, there is no greater reward than your satisfaction.

★ ★ ★ ★ ★

Thank you!
Bon Appetit, cheers, and much health!

Made in the USA
Monee, IL
21 January 2021